A Day in the Life of a...

Teacher

Carol Watson

W
FRANKLIN WATTS
LONDON•SYDNEY

Sonia Harvey is an infant
school teacher.
At 7.30 a.m. she arrives
at school and starts
preparing the classroom
for the day ahead.

At 8.50 a.m. Mrs Harvey asks the school children to line up in the playground.

Mrs Harvey greets her class and shows the children into the school.

3

"Time for the register, Year 1," says Mrs Harvey. The children sit together quietly and read their books until their names are called out.

Next Mrs Harvey takes Year 1 to join the rest of the school in the hall for assembly. "There are five birthdays today," says Mrs Westwood, the teacher in charge.

Mrs Harvey plays the piano as everyone sings.

After assembly, Mrs Harvey sets up weighing and measuring activities for some of Year 1. "How many cubes have you used, Melissa?" she asks.

Then Mrs Harvey helps the other children with their project work.

She helps Olivia on the computer. "What information can we find here?" Mrs Harvey asks.

At 10.30 a.m. it's playtime.
Mrs Harvey is on 'playground duty'.
She has a drink of coffee while she
watches over the children.

After play Year 1
have their drinks, too.

"Who wants a biscuit?"
Mrs Harvey asks.

Next Mrs Harvey
listens to her
class reading.
"Can you tell me
that word, Anand?"
she asks.

Meanwhile Mrs Mott, a helper, does an art activity with some of the children.
"Make sure you stick the hair on properly, Elliot," she says.

At 12.00 it's lunch time.
Mrs Harvey has a snack and chats with
the other teachers in the staff room.

During the break
Mrs Harvey has a
singing class with
the older children.

Then Mrs Harvey
teaches the
recorder group.
"We'll learn a
new tune, today,"
she tells them.

At 1.30 p.m. Mrs Harvey returns to her own class. There, she helps some children with a water activity and tells others how to look after Toffee, the guinea pig.

During the afternoon break
Mrs Harvey has a meeting with
Mr Jones, the headteacher.
"We need to talk about the school
concert," he says.

At the end of the afternoon, Mrs Harvey gathers the children together for a story. "And what do you think the wise owl said?" she asks.

Now it's home time. Mrs Harvey tells the children to wait for their parents to collect them.

Mrs Harvey talks to one of the mums. "Michelle has done some good work, today," she says.

17

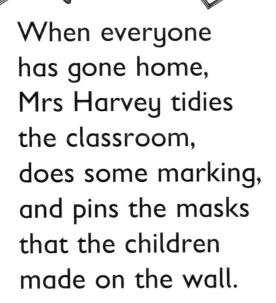

When everyone
has gone home,
Mrs Harvey tidies
the classroom,
does some marking,
and pins the masks
that the children
made on the wall.

Get your
sketchbooks
from here

Get your
maths books
from here

Now it's 5.30 p.m. and she sets off for home. "This has been a really busy day," Mrs Harvey says to herself.

How you can help your teacher

1. Be helpful and kind to other children and teachers.

2. Look after school things carefully.

3. Make sure your clothing is always marked with your name.

4. Always tell your teacher if you are worried about something.

5. Listen carefully when your teacher talks to your class.

6. Make sure you come to school on time.

Facts about teachers

There are different kinds of school teacher - Infant, Junior and Secondary. Sonia is an Infant teacher. She works at a Primary school. Her class is Year 1. Primary schools are divided into two sections - Infant and Junior. The children are grouped according to age.

Infant school

- Nursery class — 3-4 years
- Reception class — 5 years — Key Stage 1
- Year 1/middle infants — 6 years
- Year 2 — 7 years

Junior school

- Year 3/ first year junior — 8 years
- Year 4/ second year junior — 9 years — Key Stage 2
- Year 5/ third year junior — 10 years
- Year 6/ fourth year junior — 11 years

Secondary school

This is for children aged 12-18

To be a teacher you need to like children, be good at explaining things and have a good sense of humour.
You also need to be enthusiastic, organized and very patient.

23

Index

© 1998 Franklin Watts

Franklin Watts
96 Leonard Street
London EC2A 4XD

Franklin Watts Australia
56 O'Riordan Street
Alexandria, Sydney, NSW 2015

ISBN 0 7496 4102 9

Dewey Decimal Classification
Number 371

10 9 8 7 6 5 4

Editor: Samantha Armstrong
Design: Kirstie Billingham
Photography: Steve Shott
Illustration: Kim Woolley

With thanks to Sonia Harvey,
Adjoa Ezekwe, Gwynne Jones
and all the staff and children at
Grove Park Primary School,
Chiswick, London.

A CIP catalogue record for this
book is available from the British
Library.

Printed in Malaysia

READABOUT

Wheels

This edition 2003

Franklin Watts
96 Leonard Street
London EC2A 4XD

Franklin Watts Australia
45-51 Huntley Street
Alexandria
NSW 2015

Editor: Ambreen Husain
Design: K and Co

The Publisher and Photographer would like to
thank
Motosport of Cranleigh, Surrey, for their kind
help and assistance.

Additional Photographs:
Austin J Brown/APL pp. 22-23; Eye Ubiquitous p.
27

A CIP catalogue record for this book is available
from the British Library.

ISBN 0 7496 5276 4

Printed in Hong Kong

READABOUT
Wheels

Text: Henry Pluckrose
Photography: Chris Fairclough

FRANKLIN WATTS
LONDON•SYDNEY

What do you need
to make this bike work?

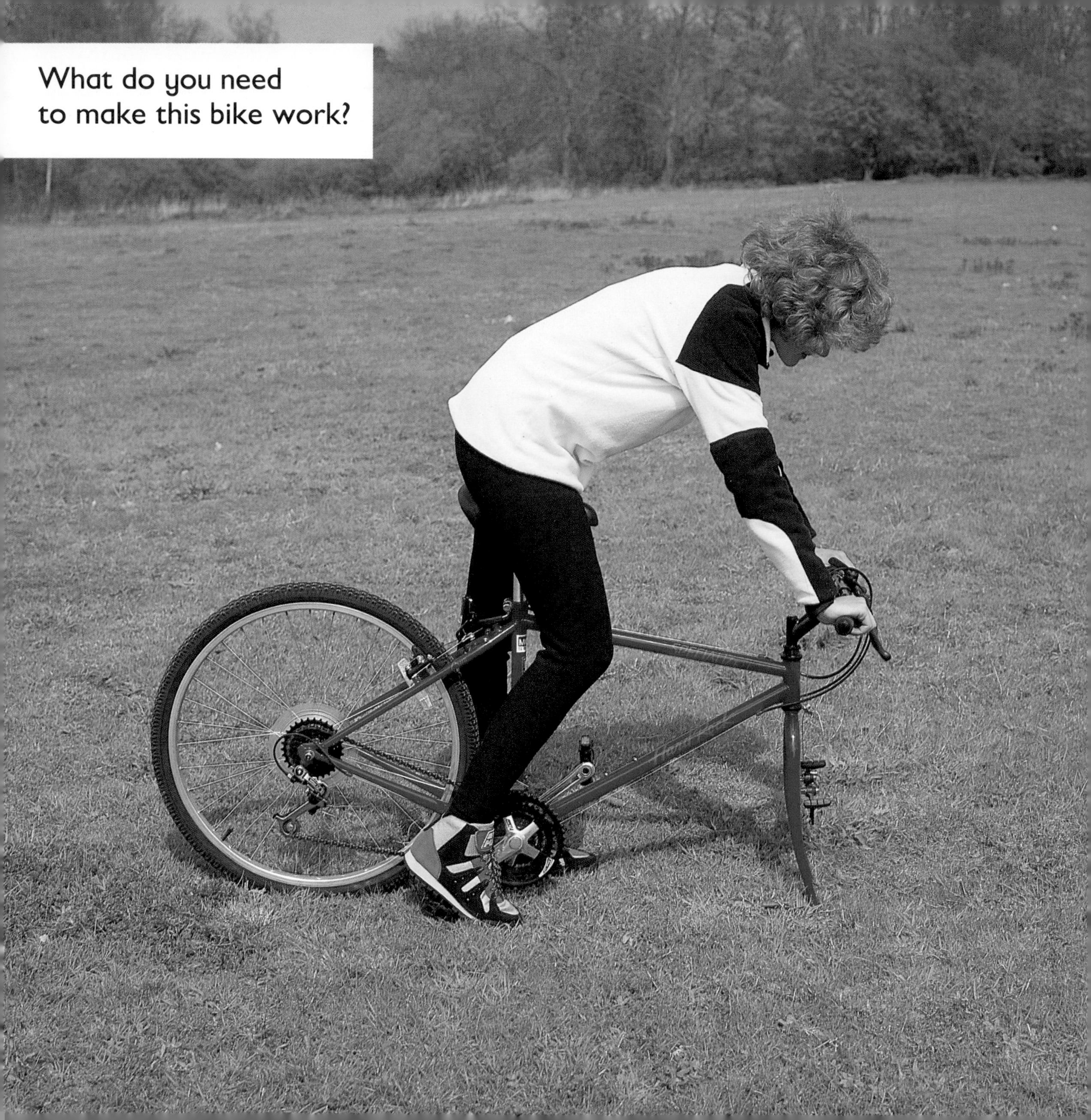

What happens to the wheels when you push the pedals?

Wheels are made in many sizes.

All wheels are the
same shape.
You could not have a
square wheel
or one shaped like a triangle.

The centre of a wheel
is called the hub.
A wheel turns on an axle.
The axle fits into the hub.

The hub is joined
to the circular rim —
sometimes by thin spokes
and sometimes by thick
pieces of wood or metal.

Some wheels are made of wood.
They wear out quickly.
To make them last longer
a metal strip is fitted round
the rim.

The tyres of buses, lorries and cars are made of steel and thick rubber.
The steel gives the tyre its shape and makes it strong.

When you blow up a balloon
the rubber feels hard
because the balloon
is packed with air.
When a tyre is fitted to a
wheel air is pumped into it
to make it hard.

Rubber tyres have a pattern
called a tread.
The tread helps the tyre
to grip the road.

Some wheels need a special
kind of tread.
The pattern of this tread
helps the tractor to move
on soft and muddy earth.

Sometimes even the wheels
of a tractor can get stuck.
The wheels on this earthmover
turn inside a track.
They run on their own road!

Sometimes, when the roads are covered with ice and snow, chains are fitted around tyres.
The chains grip the icy road and the wheels turn without slipping.

Where else do you find wheels?
There are wheels on aircraft…

and on caravans and
motorcycles.

There are wheels on shoes and on suitcases.

Chairs can also have wheels.

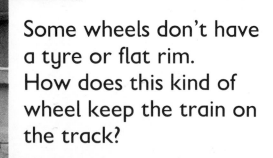

Some wheels don't have a tyre or flat rim. How does this kind of wheel keep the train on the track?

How many wheels can you find in this picture?

This wheel has teeth
cut around the rim.
It is called a cog wheel.

The teeth in one cog wheel
fit into the teeth of the
cog wheel next to it.
When the first wheel turns
the next wheel turns too.

Where can you find
cog wheels like this?
What happens when
the cog wheels turn?

This is a water wheel.
When water falls on the wheel
the wheel turns.
The turning wheel
drives machinery
inside the mill.

Wheels are used to
steer buses and boats...

and to have fun.

Wheels are used in many different ways.
What would life be like without wheels?

About this book

All books which are specially prepared for young children are written to meet the interest of the age group at which they are directed. This may mean presenting an idea in a humorous or unconventional way so that ideas which hitherto have been grasped somewhat hazily are given sharper focus. The books in this series aim to bring into focus some of the elements of life and living which we as adults tend to take for granted.

This book develops and explores an idea using simple text and thought-provoking photographs. The words will encourage questioning and discussion – whether they are read by adult or child. Children enjoy having information books read to them just as much as stories and poetry. The younger child may ignore the written words ... pictures play an important part in learning, particularly if they encourage talk and visual discrimination.

Young children acquire much information in an incidental, almost random fashion. Indeed, they learn much just by being alive! The adult who uses books like this one needs to be sympathetic and understanding of the young child's intellectual development.
It offers a particular way of looking, an approach to questioning which will result in talk, rather than 'correct' one word answers.

Henry Pluckrose